CCSS Genre Myth

MW00570729

Essential Question
What do myths help us understand?

Hercules *and the* Golden Apples

adapted by Betsy Hebert
illustrated by Yevgenia Nayberg

CHAPTER 1 Hercules

Long ago in Greece, a powerful hero lived. His name was Hercules, and he was the son of the mighty god Zeus.

Even as a baby, Hercules had great strength. As a man, he was stronger than any other.

But the goddess Hera did not like Hercules. She cursed the strong man and caused him to go crazy. Hercules did terrible things in his madness.

At last, Hercules returned to normal.
He saw the damage he had done, and
he begged for forgiveness. He asked the
gods to let him earn back his honor.

The gods agreed and sent him to work
for a king. The king gave Hercules twelve
very difficult tasks to perform. He disliked
Hercules, and he wanted the hero to fail.

No one thought Hercules could complete all twelve tasks. They seemed impossible. But Hercules did complete them, one by one. He used all of his strength and many tricks, and he refused to give up.

This is the story of one of those tasks.

2 Looking

The king was a weak and greedy man. He wanted three of Hera's golden apples, but he knew he could not get them himself. He gave Hercules the task of finding them.

The apples were not just golden in color. They were made of gold, and they had special powers. The tree had been a wedding gift to Hera from Mother Earth.

Hera loved the tree and kept it hidden in a secret garden. Three nymphs, or nature spirits, guarded the tree. A dragon with many heads lay below as the leaves rustled.

Only one person on Earth knew where to find the garden. That was Nereus, the old man of the sea. Hercules found the sea god and grabbed him. Nereus did not want to tell where the garden was.

So Hercules squeezed Nereus tighter. Nereus used his own powers. He changed into many different animals and tried to get away. But Hercules held the sea god firmly. Finally, the old man told Hercules what he needed to know.

On his way to the garden, Hercules heard mighty groans. It was the Titan god Prometheus, chained to a rock by Zeus. Every day, an eagle appeared to peck the giant god.

Hercules felt sorry for Prometheus and set him free. To thank Hercules, Prometheus told him not to pick Hera's apples himself. Only a god could touch the apples and live.

CHAPTER 3 Finding

Hercules traveled over land and sea to the edge of the earth. Finally, he came to the secret garden. But how could he pick the apples?

Nearby, Hercules saw the Titan Atlas. This god had been forced by Zeus to hold the world on his shoulders.

Hercules formed a plan to trick Atlas. He offered to hold the world while the god picked three apples.

Atlas quickly agreed, but he feared the dragon. He asked Hercules to kill the beast.

Hercules drew his bow and shot the creature, and then he took the world from Atlas. The nymphs guarding the tree begged and cried, but Atlas picked the shining apples. Then he refused to take the world back from Hercules.

4 Tricking

But Hercules was ready. "Very well," he said to Atlas. "I will hold the world while you take the apples to the king. But first I need to make a pad for my shoulders. This world is very hard and heavy. Will you hold it while I get ready?"

Atlas agreed. He put down the apples and took the weight of the world again. "Thank you," Hercules said, and he hurried off with the apples.

Hercules gave the apples to the king. But the king was afraid of making Hera angry. He gave the apples back to Hercules! The goddess Athena agreed to return the apples to the garden.

And so Hercules completed another task. He was one step closer to gaining forgiveness and honor.

Respond to Reading

Summarize

Use important details to summarize what happens in *Hercules and the Golden Apples.*

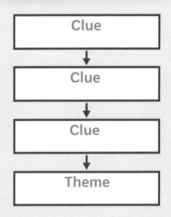

Text Evidence

1. How do you know *Hercules and the Golden Apples* is a myth? Genre

2. What is the overall idea this myth tells about? Theme

3. Use sentence clues to figure out the meaning of *tasks* on page 4.

   Sentence Clues

4. Write about what was special about the golden apples. Give details about how they affected people. Write About Reading

Compare Texts
Read about real apples.

Apples

Apples grow on trees all over the world. Apples can be red, yellow, or green. They can taste sweet or tart.

This tree grows yellow apples called Golden Delicious.

A group of apple trees is called an orchard.

Look at the different parts of an apple.

An apple grows in stages. First, a bud forms on the tree. In spring, the bud blooms into a flower. Part of the flower will develop and grow into an apple.

Most apples are grown from a process called grafting. A farmer follows steps:

1. Cut a bud from a tree.
2. Make a cut in the bark of another tree.
3. Peel back the bark.
4. Put the bud's stem under the bark.
5. Tape the bud and bark together.

Apples are a healthful snack.

People have eaten apples since prehistoric times. Apples probably grew first in southwest Asia. Colonists brought apples with them to America. They are one of the world's favorite crops.

Today, China grows the most apples, and the United States is the second-biggest apple grower. It grows about 5 million tons of apples per year.

Make Connections

What can we learn from the myth of Hercules? Essential Question

How are real apples different from Hera's apples? Text to Text

Focus on
Genre

Myth A myth is a type of folktale. It might tell a story about gods or goddesses. It might tell how something came to be.

What to Look for In *Hercules and the Golden Apples,* Hercules is god-like because he is so strong. Atlas holds the whole world on his shoulders. Hera's apple tree grows apples that are made of gold.

Your Turn

Plan your own myth about a god or goddess. Give your character a name and tell what powers he or she has. Write where the story takes place and what your character needs to find or do.